EX LIBRIS

BECOME ALL FLAME
LENT WITH AFRICAN SAINTS

FR. DEACON JOHN R. GRESHAM, JR.

PARK END BOOKS

SUGAR LAND
2022

Cover image "Surrender" Copyright © Steve Prince
Interior Icon Drawings: Andrew Kinard
Interior Icon Drawings Copyright © Andrew Kinard
Cover & Book Design: Summer Kinard

Publisher's Cataloging-in-Publication Data

Names: Gresham, Jr., Fr. Deacon John R., 1966- author.
Title: Become all flame: lent with African saints / written by Fr.
Deacon John R. Gresham, Jr.; cover image by Steve Prince;
illustrations by Andrew Kinard; design by Summer Kinard
Description: Sugar Land [Texas]: Park End Books, 2022.
Identifiers: ISBN: 978-1-953427-21-2
Subjects: Religion – Christianity – Saints & Sainthood, Religion –
Christianity – Orthodox
Library of Congress Control Number: 2022901532

www.parkendbooks.com

Memory Eternal
The Reverend Carter Randolph Wicks
My wise elder of the faith

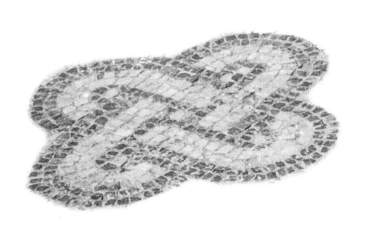

✝ABLE OF CONTENTS

USEFUL TERMS

THEOTOKOS: The title (Mother of God) given from the time of the earliest prayers of the Church to the Mother of God, the blessed Virgin Mary.

ABBA: An honorary name for a wise elder or Desert Father. It means "Father."

AMMA: An honorary name for a wise elder or Desert Mother. It means "Mother."

MARTYR: A Christian who bore witness to Christ unto death, refusing to renounce Christ even when subjected to tortures and murder. Martyr means "witness," because the unfailing faith of those killed for the sake of Christ bore witness to their belief in His Resurrection.

ASCETIC: Asceticism means "struggle," and an ascetic is one who disciplines himself or herself to crucify the desires of their flesh so that they might more fully devote themselves to the life of the spirit and prayer with the Holy Spirit.

DIVINE LITURGY: This is the name for the primary church service of the ancient and Orthodox Church. Also known as the Eucharist ("thanksgiving") or Mass ("sacrifice") the Divine Liturgy is when Christians take Communion and experience the full presence of Christ on earth. It is called heaven on earth for this reason.

MONASTIC: From the word for single, or solitary, a monastic (a monk or a nun) dedicates themselves wholly to God through

1

vows of celibacy, poverty, obedience, and usually group disciplines of daily prayer and life called a monastic Rule.

PERSECUTIONS: These refer to various waves of violence and seeking out Christians for punishment as atheists (for not believing in the Roman pantheon of gods) in the Roman Empire, primarily before 313, when the Edict of Milan issued by Constantine made Christianity one of the legal religions in the Roman Empire. During a wave of persecution, officials would crack down on what they saw as Christian impiety against common order when Christians refused to participate in public festivals or to show honor to the emperor and the local deities through sacrifices. Christian impiety towards the idols seemed to the Roman leaders to be acts of subversion of the Empire's stability and authority, because the Romans saw their power as coming from their gods. As a result, they would seek out and kill dissidents like the Christians in what were usually regional persecutions and sometimes widespread under particular leaders like Decius and Diocletian.

PAGAN: This is the name Christians use to refer to the folk piety of the ancient Romans and other neighbors who worshipped idols. It's from the word for "countryside" because it reflects the homegrown, usually localized, and native piety in the areas in which the Gospel spread.

FORNICATION: This term refers to any sexual activity that uses oneself or another person dishonorably, as objects for fulfilling greed or will to power or mere bodily desires rather than honorable intercourse in marriage and recognizing the dignity of the image of God in one another.

REPOSED: When a Christian dies, we say they have reposed, or fallen asleep, in the Lord, because Christ has already trampled down death by death, bestowing life on those in the tombs.

ACKNOWLEDGEMENTS

ALL PRAISES TO GOD; the Father, Son, and Holy Spirit. Thank you, St. Cyprian of Carthage for patiently waiting for me to come to the Orthodox Christian Faith. Metropolitan Joseph, Bishop Thomas, and Archpriest James for their blessings.

Mr. & Mrs. Deacons John R. Gresham, Sr. taught me to pursue God with all seriousness. My many friends and relatives who put up with my peculiarities.

Prayers and thanks to Brenda who prays with me daily. Your patience is amazing.

The African American Baptists who introduced me to Jesus Christ. The Fellowship of St. Moses the Black who invited me to deeper spiritual growth. Saint Basil the Great Antiochian Orthodox Church for giving me a place to grow.

FOREWORD

I HAD BEEN READING Fr. Deacon John's blog posts on African saints for many months when I felt convicted that his unique perspective on these beloved saints deserved a wider audience. Not only was Fr. Deacon John bringing forward the wisdom and examples of holy men and women whose lives and continuing prayers had rooted and watered the Church for centuries, but he was teaching as someone who knows in his bones what it means to be Black and holy. These saints are grafted close to the trunk of the Vine of Christ that roots us all. Fr. Deacon John's eyes-open teaching of their stories is the fruit of their lives and an offering for us to likewise imitate them as they imitate Christ, to bear the fruit of the Holy Spirit in our lives, too.

I am a Christian today because of St. Augustine, one of the better-known saints in this book. When I first encountered St. Augustine, I was a trauma-surviving, battered hearted nineteen-year-old, sitting in my first church history class, frustrated that the formulaic faith of my childhood didn't hold up to proofs. What had looked good on paper as a map to get me out of the hell I had grown up in, seemed like a fairy tale as soon as I had space to breathe. I hadn't lost my faith, but I sure felt lost. It was only with half an ear that I heard the professor start his lecture on St. Augustine and the inspiration of scripture. Half an ear was enough for God, though, for He sent me a word in season while I was right there in my weariness.

As I stared out the window at the construction equipment moving through the drizzly day, my professor said, "The Bible is like a window. The Holy Spirit doesn't want you to look at the glass, but He pours light and inspiration through it." That one lecture on St. Augustine's view of the Living Word was like a wind that blew all the leaves off the path God had laid at my feet. I could see my way again, the way of Christ, not formulaic but living, not dead and contained, but alive and spreading and calling me into life.

I recognized that same gift of a word in season when I read Fr. Deacon John's meditations. I made the sign of the Cross, asked God and the saints (especially St. Augustine and St. Anthony) for help, and wrote to Fr. Deacon John to ask him to prayerfully consider writing a Lenten devotional for our press so that we might sow these encouraging stories wider. Thank the Lord, after reflecting and gaining permission from his hierarchy, Fr. Deacon John said yes.

As Fr. Deacon John relates in his introduction, this book is not exhaustive; there are many more African saints than the hundred or so featured in the forty-nine daily entries of this devotional. I drew the title from a conversation between two such saints, the desert ascetics Abba Joseph and Abba Lot. (If you wish to supplement your reading on African Saints beyond this book this Lent, I encourage you to find a volume of *The Sayings of the Desert Fathers*, which is listed in the bibliography and referenced in several places throughout this volume.) In their conversation about the goal of their prayer and disciplined lives, the older man Abba Joseph raised his hands to the sky so that his fingers became like fire, and he said, "If you will, you can become all flame." It was this evocative image of the desire for God that through discipline and virtue and prayer and sacraments could transform the very bodies of the people most consumed by love for God that inspired the title.

I saw an echo of that long-ago moment of transformation in the artist Steve Prince's image "Surrender," with its dignity and grace and clear communion with God. I saw in the African American man in a tee shirt the African Abba in his raffia robe, both embodying the holiness of life in Christ. Some elements of the lives of the saints in this book are unsettling or foreign to our modern sensibilities, but they are all arranged along the same lines of the cover image, "Surrender," and the Abba with the hands of fire. They each show a little of what happens when the love of Christ constrains a person to walk through their daily habits of prayer and study and care for others into the fire of the Holy Spirit. I believe that reading these passages with a heart set on loving Christ will build the flame of love in readers, too.

These lives and meditations are arranged into seven weeks to support a daily reading habit for Orthodox Christian Great Lent, but my hope is that you will take up and read them as soon as they come to hand. We have included some representative line drawings based on Orthodox Christian icons (holy images) of the saints. Because black line drawings on light paper subtly whitewash the subjects, I have reversed the contrast in the examples here, so that the saints register more quickly as Black and viewers more readily see their outlines as shining the light of Christ. In these images, while keeping to the Byzantine language of icons, we have restored the African facial features and hair textures that have often been lost to the customs of iconography in European and Northern and Eastern Mediterranean regions where icons have survived. There was once a thriving iconographic and mosaic tradition across North Africa, some of which still exists in Egyptian Coptic Orthodox and Ethiopian Orthodox Christian Churches, but a great deal of which is in ruins, buried a yard or more under the farmlands of regions conquered during the Islamic migrations of the 7th and 8th Centuries.

I had a professor in seminary, Dr. Susan Keefe (May her memory be eternal!) whose asceticism and holiness were so evident that she traveled freely among all people. She went into places forbidden to others and saw treasures lost to most people. Because of Dr. Keefe, I have seen photographs of the floor mosaics where St. Augustine once preached. Her manner of grace and kindness and simplicity had impressed a farmer so much that he took her secretly into his wheat field and dug up a corner of the church for her to see.

It's in her memory and in gratitude to St. Augustine and his mother St. Monica that I have included ancient church floor mosaic patterns in many of the transitional spaces in this book. I couldn't give you the exact images of that church under the wheat field, but thankfully, the patterns repeat across the region so that I could find similar ones to feed your imagination. Peacocks, a symbol of immortality, crosses to guide every step, fish to recall Christ's miracles, were all common symbols in African churches of the Golden Age of Christianity in the 2nd through 7th Centuries, when African teachers guided the whole Church in knowledge of God's grace, in virtues, in biblical interpretation, and in understanding the divine and human natures of Christ. I call it the Golden Age not to evoke nostalgia over its loss to legend and the violence of history, but because it was so rich that it was like a plentiful field of ripe grain whose seed is still bearing fruit now.

Here in these pages, you will find some of the saints whose blood and prayers nourish you. If we know their lifespan or the date of their martyrdom or death, it is listed under their name. Fr. Deacon John has offered a brief description of each saint's life, often with a short admonition on how best to imitate the saint. In addition, he has written a poetic meditation that can help you pray with this saint to learn more of Christ, who is glorious in His saints. Following each of these prayers, Fr. Deacon John has listed scriptures for you to read that will help you connect the saint with the scriptures they illuminated with their lives.

It is my prayer that these devotional passages will help you be rooted and grounded in Christ, that you will experience the energizing life of the Holy Spirit, and that this work of bringing forward African saints will be blessed by Christ to heal in some measure the great wounds that racism has inflicted on the Church and the whole world. For do not misunderstand this book as neutral. It is no more neutral than the surgeon's healing knife or the insulin for a diabetic or salve to a wound or the Medicine of Immortality that heals and discomfits everyone who receives at Christ's table. This God of peace whom we serve is also the God of Truth. They cannot be separated if we are to tell the story of Christ and His Saints with the help of the Spirit of Truth. By publishing this book, we at Park End Books join with these great saints who by the power of God and lives lived in prayer and imitation and communion with Christ, defeated the devil and trampled him under their feet, as we pray that the death knell of racism will sound out in our lifetime.

Maranatha. O Lord, come.

In Christ,
Summer Kinard, M.Div., Th.M.
Senior Editor, Park End Books
Feast of St. Bessarion the Great, 2022

INTRODUCTION:
RECLAIMING OUR PLACE AT THE †ABLE

PROBABLY ONE OF THE SADDEST missed opportunities of evangelism between African Americans and the Orthodox Christian world happened around the time of the World's Fair in 1893 (see, "The Pain of Missed Opportunities" in the *Desert Fathers Dispatch* blog, April 27th, 2014). AME Bishop Daniel Payne met with Eastern Orthodox bishops and other clergy from various parts of the world who told him that the Church had African saints from the times of the Apostles. This African American educator and missionary would die a few months later with Orthodox clergy in America denying that such saints existed.

I wrote this book to remedy that misconception so that African American Christians and all Orthodox Christians will have a ready means to access some of the rich and ancient witness of African saints. I offer this work not as a complete list of every holy man and woman born on the southern shore of the Mediterranean Sea and southward. Nor do I give any detailed proof that all of these people had a dark skin pigmentation. However, in each case, the selected saints were not identified by any of my sources as coming from a Greek, Roman, or Syrian family. These are all native-born people of Carthage, Egypt, and the Upper Egyptian region of Thebes.

Greeks and Romans controlled the power throughout Northern and North Eastern Africa. Yet, they were a minority concentrated more in cities like Alexandria and Carthage. Native black Africans declined in number due to invasions from the Hyksos, Assyrians, Persians, Macedonians, and Romans. The majority of the population was an ethnic mixture of black Africans, Asiatics, and Southern Europeans. As in the modern African diaspora, a native African in the Greco Roman world could have had almost pale skin, very dark skin, or (most likely) some shade or another of a brown complexion. Using the standard of one drop of African blood made one a Negro, these saints would have been and can be considered black.

Identifying these saints as having brown pigmentation shouldn't be a shock to the Orthodox world. Our Lady of Częstochowa (one of the most beloved icons in Poland) shows the Theotokos and Christ child as dark skinned. There is no shortage of Russian and some Antiochian icons depicting a brown Lord Jesus Christ and His Mother. In areas of Germany, France, and Switzerland, Saint Maurice of Thebes is depicted as a black man in chain mail armor. As African Americans are learning more about Orthodox Christianity, we are looking for those icons of saints that look like us. Those who take up iconography are writing holy images showing native born Africans looking like black people. You will see a few of these saints represented in iconographic line drawings for the headings of each week in this book.

These African saints remind us of the universal nature of the Christian faith. Our faith was born in the Levant region that was the crossroads of cultures.

Pentecost was not the only day that people from all over the known world came to Jerusalem. Djan Darada was an Ethiopian official who came to worship there. Rome sent a native Italian legion to Joppa. Greek and Latin were the languages of commerce, education, and government in the Eastern and Western portions of the Empire. However, Ancient African Punic, Coptic, and Nubian languages were still common. Also, Aramaic, Armenian, and Syriac were spoken by common people. There were other European languages represented in the early centuries of the Church as well. What brought everyone together was that the truth of the Gospel spoke to all people of all ethnicities. To say that all ancient Christians looked the same is an injustice to the God who so loved the world and a Savior who will bring forth a great multitude from every nation, race, and language.

Failing to reveal the African saints has added to the idea of Christianity being a "white man's religion." Protestantism has severed us from the likes of Carthaginian martyrs, the Desert Fathers, and Christian Nubia. Belief systems such as the Moorish Science Temple, Hebrew Israelites, and others have quickly filled the void with their sometimes spurious teachings of the African American's ancient past. Denouncing their historical errors means nothing unless we are providing the stories of the early holy Christian men and women (saints) and being honest about where they came from and what they may have looked like. The natives of Upper Egypt to the Nubian border were far more likely to be black or brown than pure Greek or Roman. Christianity came to this region by way of some of the earliest Apostles and monastics long before the birth of Constantine. Even under his rule, the Desert Fathers did not use Christianity as a weapon of imperial force or domination. These men and women struggled against their own passions; striving to build a home in God's kingdom rather than violently establish one in the world.

Even more than skin color, the African saints offer incredible stories of faith and spiritual growth that aren't found in the "Bible alone" and "all I need is Jesus" ministries of our time. What does it look like to actually be tortured and die for the faith? Perpetua and Felicity's narrative gives us a look into the strong will it takes to face down being sentenced to barbaric coliseum games for the sake of Christ. Can a person live with few earthly possessions and focus only on the ways of God? Macarius the Great helped a burglar steal his stuff as he caught the man breaking into his modest hut. "Christian" has become more of a label than a way of life in our modern world. Stories of the saints from all parts of the world can help remind us to think and live differently. I offer these stories of our forebears in the faith along with brief teachings on how we can receive their witness today in the hopes that they will expand our imagination of what holy faces look like and make plain the paths we can walk to imitate them.

Fr. Deacon John R. Gresham
January 2022

WEEK ONE

ST. SIMON OF CYRENE

SIMON OF CYRENE
(SIMEON CALLED NIGER)
1ST CENTURY

THOUGH HE CARRIED Jesus' cross, this saint is not as well-known as others from the African continent. Yet, his place among the holy men can be described in one word: compelled. According to the synoptic Gospels, this was involuntary, as the Romans forced this passer-by to carry the cross for Jesus Christ up Mount Calvary for the crucifixion. The compulsion became voluntary as he remained in Jerusalem and bore witness to the resurrection and Pentecost. When a group of believers fled to Antioch, Simon was among the Cyrenians who began preaching the Gospel to Greeks and Jews. In this Christian community, he became part of the clergy and was known as Simeon Niger. By his name, many Christians accept that Simon was a black African.

There was a time that many parents and grandparents took and made boys and girls go to church. This sort of compulsion is good to the degree of training up children in the faith. Yet, true love for Christ and spiritual maturity is not found in this involuntary training, no matter how good the intentions. It is only when we encounter the Lord for ourselves and feel called to share our faith that our self-compulsion shows our love for the Lord. May this voluntary compulsion borne of love be on us all.

MEDITATION

Your role on Calvary's Mountain is not lost on us
For on your back, you took up the cross of our God
Priestly Simon, pray that we will have the strength and
    resolve
To so deny ourselves and follow Christ always.

Matthew 27:32, Mark 15:21-22, Luke 23:26,
Acts 11:19-21, 13:1

SCILLITAN MARTYRS
JULY 17, 180

CARTHAGE AND ROME fought three bitter wars from 264 to 146 BC for control of the western Mediterranean. In the end, the Romans mercilessly sacked the African city, and tens of thousands of people were enslaved. The city of Carthage was rebuilt by 40 BC and became the second largest city in the western half of the Empire. It was common for some Carthaginians, Numidians and Punics to become Roman citizens. However, resistance and resentment toward their occupiers continued. Taking up arms and re-establishing Hannibal's kingdom was impossible. Hearing the Gospel from St. Photini (the "Woman at the Well" in John 4:1-28) and others, Africans dissatisfied with their earthly kingdom put their hopes in the eternal kingdom through Jesus Christ.

Scilli, a small town outside of Carthage, didn't have many Christian writings. A group of believers there, having little more than a few of Paul's epistles, preferred death in the name of the Lord than to submit to Roman orders of how and whom to worship. *The Acts of the Scillitan Martyrs* is one of the oldest official documents dealing with Christianity in Africa written in Latin.

Renounce the world and worship God alone. His kingdom is greater than any this world can offer.

MEDITATION

The governor's decree sentenced you to death in this
world.

Yet, you didn't cower or tremble in fear.

His words gave your heart reason to celebrate.

The shedding of your blood led you to glory in the world
to come.

Matthew 10:28, Mark 8:37, 38

ASCLAS OF EGYPT
287

JESUS CHRIST WAS TAKEN to Egypt by Joseph and Mary, having been directed to do so by God (Matthew 2:13-15). The Apostle and Evangelist Mark established the Church there before his brutal martyrdom. As with Carthage, the faith did not become the sole possession of a few major urban centers on the Mediterranean Sea. The Gospel was preached to the upper reaches of the Nile River into Nubia and Ethiopia.

Asclas was born in the Middle Egyptian town of Hermopolis. He suffered horrific tortures under Emperor Diocletian for not abandoning the Christian faith. His tormentors assumed he was near death. But the saint was calmly enduring their barbaric acts.

The local governor was taking Asclas to a town across the Nile when the boat was stopped in the middle of the river. It would not move until the governor confessed that there was only one true God. He did, and they continued on their journey, only for the governor to continue to have the saint tortured further. Finally, they had Asclas tied to a large stone and drowned in the Nile. As he was sentenced, Asclas urged the Christians with him to continue to strive for God's rewards.

MEDITATION

The earthly ruler made a false confession to trick Asclas
But the truly confessing Egyptian had the power of great
endurance to the end.
Even as the Nile's waters slowly stole his breath
Asclas encouraged more believers to follow Christ.

Acts 7:54-59

✝HEODORA AND DIDYMUS THE SOLDIER
MAY 27, 303 OR 304

AMONG THE CRUELEST tortures the enemies of Christ inflicted on believers was rape. Both men and women sought to keep themselves sexually pure, offering their bodies to holiness. Even being married and having children was not as important to some believers as life-long celibacy, although all weren't called to such a life.

During the persecution of Emperor Diocletian, the maiden Theodora confessed to the judge that she renounced marriage in order to be a bride of Christ. The wicked man had her sent to a brothel to be assaulted. While some men were arguing over who would take her first, Didymus dressed as a soldier and chased them away. Taking the virgin into a room, he had her dress in his clothing so she could escape. Eventually, He was arrested and confessed his Christian faith and what he did. The judge sentenced him to be executed. When Theodora learned of her rescuer's fate, she came to the executioner and asked to die with Didymus. They were both beheaded and their bodies burned.

Do not be led astray by our oversexed society. Virginity and chastity are virtues worth protecting with our own lives. Believing in Christ means believing that members of Christ's Body are sacred, too.

MEDITATION

Didymus, protector of virtue
Would not allow his virgin sister to be treated
    shamelessly.
Theodora not standing by to let her brother perish alone
Joined him in the celebration of martyred souls.

Matthew 5:27-30, 19:11-12, I Corinthians 6:12-20, 7:1-9

BISHOP CYPRIAN OF CARTHAGE
AUGUST 31, 258

ONE OF THE REASONS why the Gospel of Jesus Christ attracted so many people of Carthage was the promise of a greater kingdom than Rome. The pagan-born Cyprian had no problem expressing his renunciation of the world after he became a Christian. In a letter to another believer, he denounced the imperial army as a band of robbers and the navy as pirates. He also bemoaned the sexual promiscuity in society as well. The bishop encouraged his flock to live as virtuous lights in a world of darkness.

Cyprian was a very forgiving leader of the Church, as well. Sometimes Christians gave in to Roman authorities and made offerings to the emperor, renouncing their faith in Jesus to save themselves from death or torture. A party of believers, the Donatists, declared that anyone who betrayed the Lord was unable to return to the Church. The bishop considered this renunciation (called apostasy) a very serious matter. However, he taught that such Christians could be readmitted to the body of believers over time and if they were truly repentant. For Christ came not to call the righteous, but sinners to repentance.

Though Cyprian managed to evade arrest during one wave of persecution, eventually he received a death sentence for his faith in Christ. Before being beheaded, he gave the executioner a bag of gold coins.

Seek a higher spiritual way of living than what the world offers. God forgives all who earnestly repent.

MEDITATION

Pillar of Carthage
Point the way to the open door of repentance.
Holy Cyprian, let me be hidden in the depths of the
    Gospel truth
Until I must stand on the day of my judgement.

Acts 2:38 40, Matthew 7:13, Luke 12:8 10

IRADIA

(RHAIS)

SEPTEMBER 23, 308

THE ROMAN IMPERIAL GOVERNMENT thought that by persecuting and executing Christians that the church would die off. No one, they thought, would want to join a religious movement in which being a member could be brutally punished. Also, there was no earthly kingdom that could save the lives of arrested believers. Yet, the early believers in Jesus Christ willingly chose punishment in this world for the sake of the world to come. Even more so, observers of their courage in the face of tortures and death were moved with admiration. Many of them readily cried out, "I too am a Christian," and also became martyrs.

Iradia was drawing water in her little Egyptian village when she saw a boat sailing by with Christians on their way to be executed. Although the Roman officers had no reason to seek her out and arrest her, she voluntarily asked to join the condemned believers. They made their way to Antinopolis where they were tortured and killed. Iradia was beheaded.

MEDITATION

Iradia, let me go with you.

May I also bear the cross.

Suffering and death to this world are a small price to pay.

There is great reward on the other side of the river.

Matthew 19:27-29, I Peter 3:12, 13, Revelation 2:10

CALLISTRATUS AND 49 COMPANIONS
SEPTEMBER 27, 304

SOMETIMES PEOPLE HEAR stories of how their ancestors were faithful to Christ after seeing a great miracle. Callistratus, a Carthaginian soldier in the Roman army, was one such believer. His grandfather, Neokorus, also served for Rome and was sent to Judea. While there, he was assigned to guard the tomb of the recently crucified "Jesus, King of the Jews." Early on Sunday morning, he was surprised to see the dead man rise up from the tomb. He learned more about Jesus by keeping company with the apostles and returned to Carthage, helping to spread the Gospel.

Callistratus believed his grandfather Neokorus' stories and became a Christian even though other soldiers in his unit were pagan. One night, his fellows spied on him as he prayed to Jesus without mentioning any other God. He was arrested, tortured, and bound in a bag and drowned in the sea. But, the bag struck a rock and Callistratus rode on a dolphin back to dry land alive. Seeing this miracle, 49 of his fellow soldiers proclaimed their faith in Jesus Christ. After more tortures, they were cut to pieces.

MEDITATION

Callistratus learned the faith from his grandfather.
My soul, listen to our foreparents.
May I also be a soldier for the Lord
Even to die for the battlefield of prayer.

Matthew 24:9, 13, 28:11-15

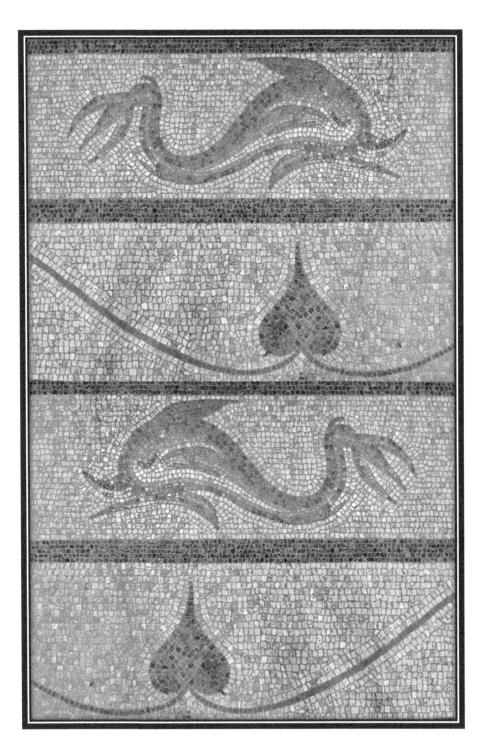

WEEK ✝WO

S✝. ᴆJAN ᴆARAᴅA

DJAN DARADA
(THE ETHIOPIAN EUNUCH)
JANUARY 4TH, 1ST CENTURY

ETHIOPIA HAS HAD CONTACTS with Israelites and Jews dating back to the Old Testament period. The most well-known encounter was that of the Queen of Sheba visiting King Solomon (I Kings/III Kingdoms 10:1 13). As a result, communities of Ethiopians learned to worship the God of Israel. Djan Darada was devout enough to make a pilgrimage to Jerusalem. Being a man of high rank, he was able to have a copy of the scriptures to read during the journey.

As the eunuch read aloud, the Lord directed Philip to run alongside his chariot close enough to hear. Only after being invited to join him and explain the scriptures did Philip share the Gospel with Djan Darada. Being convinced that Jesus was the Son of God and not wanting to waste any time, he asked that Philip would baptize him as they came to a body of water. He continued back to Ethiopia, where he was martyred. The Ethiopian Tewahedo Orthodox Church recognizes this saint as an early forerunner.

We should make the effort to worship the Lord. Along with this, we should continue reading the scriptures and spiritual books. Ask experienced believers to help us understand what we do not, and act quickly on our encounters with the Lord and His people.

MEDITATION

Trusted leader in the African queen's court
The Lord has entrusted you to receive instruction in the truth.

Let me not waste time in the hearing of the Gospel;
Like Djan Darada, let me rejoice in His death and Resurrection.

Psalm 68:31, Acts 8:26-40

MENAS

(MINA)

NOVEMBER 11, 304

MENAS WAS AN EGYPTIAN who became a soldier in the Roman Army. Known for valor and courage, he became a favorite commander of the imperial officials. This was during the time of Diocletian's great persecution of Christians. They ordered Menas to assist in persecuting Christians in Asia Minor. Menas refused to be a part of it and withdrew to a wilderness to focus on a life of prayer. Yet, the bold soldier came back to the place he had fled. His commander offered to return Menas to his previous rank if he would deny Christ. He refused and denounced the pagan believers. They brutally tortured and beheaded him. Local Christians gathered his body, and he was buried near Alexandria, where a Church would later be built in his honor.

During World War II, the Germans sought to invade and capture British-held Egypt and the oil supplies of the Middle East. They were routed at the Battle of El Alemin. Some Cypriot, Greek, and other Orthodox Christian soldiers who fought alongside the British saw a Roman soldier with a spear riding a camel, attacking the Germans. They knew it was none other than Saint Menas himself aiding them. The stories of holy men and women from ancient times remind us that God's saints still help us today in our struggles.

MEDITATION

I need the brave Menas to pray to Christ for me.
If I do, the Lord may send this soldier to fight alongside
  me.
May the enemies of my body and soul
Be defeated in the desert sands.

Acts 12:1-11, Hebrews 12:1-3,

KATHERINE

NOVEMBER 24, 310

KATHERINE WAS THE BEAUTIFUL daughter of the Roman Governor of Alexandria. She constantly turned down marriage offers from young men, desiring only to wed a man that could exceed her attractiveness and intelligence. In a dream she saw the Theotokos with the Christ child. The Lord refused to look at her, saying she was stupid and ugly. Saddened by this, Katherine sought advice from her mother, a secret Christian. She became a believer and fervently prayed that she would see the Lord's face. One night, she had the same vision. This time Jesus saw her change of heart and gave her a ring symbolizing that Katherine would be his bride.

Emperor Maximian came to Alexandria to oversee the sacrifice of Christians. Full of zeal, Katherine denounced the emperor and his high priest. They gathered 50 pagan philosophers to debate and convince the young lady that she was in the wrong. Not only did Katherine hold her ground with God's wisdom, but she convinced all of them to believe in Christ. Maximian offered to marry Katherine and grant her great fame and wealth. She angrily refused him and was subject to harsh tortures in prison. Being delivered of them all, the emperor ordered her and the 50 converts beheaded.

St. Katherine's Monastery in Egypt has one of the most famous libraries in Christianity to this day, a fitting memorial for this wise saint whose love of Christ was the highest wisdom.

MEDITATION

Lovely young martyr Katherine
Pray that I have courage not to fall to flatterers.
May my heart be the possession of the Lord alone
And my testimony be seen by generations to come.

Luke 10:38-42, Romans 1:27

†HOMAIS OF ALEXANDRIA
APRIL 13, 476

THOMAIS WAS RAISED in a pious Christian home and was known for her kind demeanor. At the age of fifteen, she married a local fisherman, and they lived in her father-in-law's home. Unfortunately, the elder's lust inflamed in him to desire the attractive young woman. Once when her husband was out fishing, the father came into her room intent on having sex with her. She fought him off, reminding him that the scriptures forbade such an act. Angry at her refusal, he threatened to kill her with a sword if she didn't give in. Standing firm not to break the commandments of God, Thomais continued her resistance. He cut her in two. The hand of God blinded the old man so that he could not see the door to leave the room. The next morning, her husband and his companions found the father bloody and his dead wife. The man confessed his grievous sin to the judge and was beheaded.

Abba Daniel of Skete had Thomais buried in a monastery near Alexandria with other monastics. When asked if this was appropriate, he replied, "She is a mother for us, for she died protecting her chastity." A young monk sought advice from this elder as he was struggling with lustful thoughts. The Abba told him to pray at the grave of Thomais. In a dream, he saw the saint telling him, "Father, accept my blessing and go in peace." He woke up the next morning free from his passions. Orthodox believers still ask for her help against sexual immorality.

MEDITATION

Against monstrous lustful passions you stood to the
    death.
Your fight for purity helped others in their soul's
    struggles.
Dear Thomais, be with me as this elder demon seeks to
    crush and kill me.
May I not compromise my commitment to the Lord.

Matthew 5:27-30, I Corinthians 6:13-20

JULIA THE VIRGIN
JULY 16, 440

JULIA WAS BORN and brought up in a Christian home in Carthage. When the city fell to the Persians, they enslaved her among other captives. A Syrian merchant owned her. He tried to convince Julia to renounce Christianity and become a pagan like himself. Failing to win her over, he dropped the matter. She was an intelligent and trustworthy servant. The master had her accompany him on various journeys.

On a trip to Gaul, the ship stopped in Corsica. The merchant and others left the ship to join in a pagan festival. Julia remained, mourning her master and the others in their worship. Local pagans saw and seized her. The merchant made only a slight protest as they carried her off to be tortured. They beat her badly, cut off her breasts, and crucified her. An angel appeared to monks on a nearby island, who took her body and buried it in the monastery church.

MEDITATION

You avoided worldliness and worthless belief
Yet the world still sought to kill you while you were
seeking to be left alone.
Julia, your hope was in the joy of the world to come with
the Lord.
May God grant this to me as I part from the ways of
delusion and death.

Ephesians 6:5, 6, Colossians 3:22

ELESBAAN

OCTOBER 24, 553

NOT EVERY NATION welcomed or tolerated Christians in their realm. Some persecuted believers as badly as the Romans before Constantine issued the Edict of Milan that granted patronage to Christians as one of the acceptable religions of the Roman Empire. King Dunaan ruled Arabia, practiced Judaism, and oppressed Christians. Elesbaan, the Axumite (ancient Ethiopian) Emperor did not tolerate the abuse of his kinsmen in faith. Urged on by the Byzantines, he waged an unsuccessful military campaign.

Curious as to why he lost the battles, he sought advice from a particular hermit. The holy man instructed him that the loss was because he sought vengeance, which belongs to the Lord alone (Hebrews 10:30). If the King would make a vow to God to give the rest of his life to prayer, he would be allowed a victory over Dunaan. Elesbaan made the promise, defeated and executed the Arabian king. He abdicated his throne and royal regalia and took on monastic garments. He lived a strict ascetic life for fifteen years until his death.

It is said that a monk who lived in the monastery where Elesbaan reposed went back on his promise to God. He began going to a tavern and getting drunk and fornicating. After a night of this debauchery, a large and hideous snake chased him. The monk tried to rebuke it

42

evoking the name of Elesbaan. However, the serpent replied, "I have been sent by an angel to devour you for not keeping your monastic vows. You have angered the Holy Spirit with your impurity and foul behavior." He repented of his wickedness and promised not to sin anymore. From that night, the monk abstained from alcohol and sexual contact. The example of a saint can condemn us. It can also be something we aspire to emulate.

MEDITATION

When you fought for your own vainglory and revenge,
    you were defeated,
But armed in humility, the Lord made you a champion.
Giving all glory to Him, you put down your crown for a
    lowly monastic cell.
Great Elesbaan, may we also grow in such grace.

Luke 9:23, I Corinthians 10:31-11:1, Revelation 3:19, 20

FULVANIUS
(MATTHEW)
NOVEMBER 16, 1ST CENTURY

AMONG THE LORD'S APOSTLES who went to other lands to spread the Gospel, Matthew went as far south as Ethiopia. According to tradition, the Lord appeared to him with a wooden rod to plant in a place to be revealed. The Apostle arrived there and did as the Lord directed. The rod grew branches and bore fruit. A fountain of water sprang up nearby. People who were ill drank the water and were healed. Many people believed the Gospel as Matthew preached to them. Platon, one of the first men he met, was ordained as the bishop of the area.

Fulvanius, a local prince, was dedicated to pagan worship and was enraged at the new religion. He had Matthew arrested and burned at a stake surrounded by his idols. Despite the amount of wood added to the fire, the Apostle was unharmed, even though the idols melted. Awestruck, the prince begged Matthew for mercy and the flames were quenched. Despite the unburned body, Matthew's spirit left to be with the Lord.

Still unsure of the phenomenon, Fulvanius had the Apostle's body put into an iron coffin and thrown into the sea. The next day, Bishop Platon and the prince saw the coffin washed up on the shore. Fulvanius deeply repented for what he had done and abdicated his throne.

The bishop baptized him and gave him the name Matthew. This Matthew later became a priest. When Platon reposed, he became the succeeding Bishop of Ethiopia.

MEDITATION

Like the Apostle Paul, you persecuted the holy in
  ignorance.
Through repentance, the Apostle Matthew's mantle was
  placed on your shoulders.
Your priesthood was a precursor to the Church in
  Ethiopia.
Holy Fulvanius, pray to the Lord that we will be blessed
  if we likewise repent.

Matthew 28:18-20, Acts 2:1-11

ST. PERPETUA

WEEK THREE

ST. FELICITY

PERPETUA AND THE CATECHUMENS SATURUS, REVOCATLUS, STATURNIUS, SECUNDULUS, AND FELICITAS OF CARTHAGE

MARCH 7, 203

IN CARTHAGINIAN SOCIETY, Perpetua and Felicity were not on the same level. The former was a noble woman while the other, a slave. However, similarities drew them together. Perpetua was nursing a baby, and Felicity was not far from giving birth. Even more so, their faith in Jesus Christ caused them to look beyond the worldly wall that would separate them and embraced each other as sisters. To be a Christian was so important to the noblewoman that she refused to deny her association with the other catechumens even after her arrest and despite the tearful pleas of her father.

While imprisoned, Perpetua saw a world beyond Carthage in the Roman Empire, in a series of prayerful visions. She envisioned her brother Christian calling to her to see what awaits the faithful. He was at the top of a great bronze ladder bordered with sharp weaponry, with a great serpent underneath, whose head became the first rung of the ladder when Perpetua invoked the protection of Christ. Arriving at the top of the ladder that represented their coming martyrdom, she saw a spacious garden and an ancient Shepherd welcoming her home with a sweet morsel from his own hand. With this

48

vision of Christ in mind, Perpetua boldly stood with her sister and brother Christians in the arena to endure harsh tortures before falling to the sword.

Through Christ, let's love each other beyond societal standards. Overcome worldly dangers and threats as God has promised us something greater in the world to come.

MEDITATION

Wicked Rome sought to shame you ladies of Carthage.
By torture in an arena they sought to shame you.
But your faith turned your afflictions into glory,
And martyrdom constructed a greater family bond.

Matthew 10:37-39, Luke 8: 20, 21, Revelation 22:1-3

ANTHONY THE GREAT

JANUARY 17, 356

A NATIVE EGYPTIAN, Anthony lost both of his parents and inherited a substantial estate while a young man. He was walking past a church when he heard the reading of the Gospel, "If you want to be perfect, sell all your possessions and give to the poor and you will have treasure in heaven, then come and follow me" (Matthew 19:21). Unlike the young ruler in the Gospel, Anthony obeyed the Lord, selling all he had and leaving his sister a portion of the estate in the care of relatives. For a while, he sought to live as an ascetic near his village. He left for the desert near the Red Sea to avoid the distractions of daily life. Here, he focused on prayer and struggling against his sinful temptations alone, with no one but God.

People were drawn to Anthony and came to him for spiritual guidance. Some decided to take up the life of a hermit looking to him as a role model. Followers collected his wisdom, which can be found in texts such as the *Sayings of the Desert Fathers*. His friend, Patriarch Athanasius, wrote *The Life of Saint Anthony the Great* not long after his death. Anthony was one of the first examples of Christian monasticism and considered to be the father of monks and nuns.

"This is the great task of man, always take blame for one's own sins and expect temptation until the day of death." -St. Anthony, from the *Sayings of the Desert Fathers*

MEDITATION

Rejecting the selfishness of the young ruler
Abba Anthony gave up all earthly things to follow
    Christ.
Father of the desert dwellers of Africa,
Pray for us lost ones of the diaspora and beyond.

Mark 1:4 to 8

MACARIUS THE GREAT

JANUARY 19, 390

THIS NATIVE EGYPTIAN worked as a camel driver before becoming one of the most well-known monastics in the Fourth Century. After the death of his wife, he began a life of ascetic struggle against his passions. Early in this effort, a young lady in a town accused him of impregnating her. Rather than claim his innocence, the monk made a great effort to weave plenty of baskets to support his new wife and child. However, she was unable to deliver the baby until she confessed that she had lain with another man. When townspeople came to apologize to him, Macarius fled even further into the desert.

Unlike Abba Anthony, Macarius was not a hermit. Unlike Abba Pachomius, he didn't set one rule for all who lived in the desert with him. His disciples built their own huts a short distance away from one another with each developing his own rule of prayer and work. They all gathered together on Saturdays for the all-night vigil and a Liturgy on Sundays. This was the "Third Way" of early monasticism.

There is a series of five morning prayers attributed to Abba Macarius in some modern Orthodox prayer books. *Fifty Spiritual Homilies of Macarius the Egyptian* are also said to be his as well. His words of wisdom and those from Macarius of Alexandria can be found in the *Sayings of the Desert Fathers.*

MEDITATION

Abba Macarius, you took the useless blows from the evil
      one,
Yet proved victorious by your great humility.
May your prayers enliven and strengthen our souls
As we commit ourselves to following Christ.

Philippians 2:5 to 11

JOHN OF THEBES

FEBRUARY 6, SIXTH CENTURY

THEBES WAS AN AREA in Upper Egypt near the border of the Roman and Nubian Empires. The people in that region were Cushites and Nubians with darker complexions than the Egyptian Copts. But, as we have seen with Simon of Cyrene, a wide variety of people of all hues could be found throughout the Greco-Roman world.

John left Egypt to worship in the Holy Land, establishing a monastery in Choziba (Hozeva) in 480. Because of his holy example of living, he was ordained Bishop of Caesarea. Preferring a simple life of ascetic discipline, John resigned and returned to the monastery he founded. He died around 525.

The Monastery of Saints John and George of Choziba (Hozeva) was attacked by Muslim Arab invaders and occupied and abandoned during the Crusades. The Greek Orthodox Patriarchate of Jerusalem re-established the monastery in the late 1870's. It is on the cliff where Abba John once lived in a cave and is said to be in the area where an ancient road connected Jerusalem to Jericho. The saint's relics remain there with a new community of monks continuing the monastic way of life.

MEDITATION

From the edge of Nubia you came to the Jericho Road
To show the hospitality of Good Samaritan.
Abba John the Theban, may the Lord reveal to us
The blessings of simplicity on earth.

Luke 10:29-37

EUGENE & MARY [MARIUS] OF ALEXANDRIA
FEBRUARY 12, 508

ONE OF THE MOST AMAZING things about monastics is their willingness to accept hardships, even those that they didn't bring on themselves. St. Mary (also known as Maria by some writers) is an example of self-denial and taking up the cross and following Christ. After her mother died, she disguised herself as a man and followed her father, Eugene, to be accepted into a men's monastery. There, she was given the name Marius.

There was an inn nearby with an innkeeper's daughter who desired to have (what she thought was) the young monk as a lover. Marius refused her advances. Angered by the rejection, the daughter lay with another man and became pregnant. She went to the monastery and accused Marius of being the father. Not revealing her real identity, Mary (as Marius) was humiliated and banished from the brotherhood. Living in an orchard outside of the monastery, she endured much suffering living alone for about three years. During that same time, her false accuser became mentally ill. Mary died, and the brother monastics then discovered the identity of Marius. The crazed innkeeper's daughter came and touched the feet of St. Mary and was healed. She confessed of the lie she told and her sin of fornication.

MEDITATION

Amma Mary, you have shown there is no male or female
    in Christ
As you stayed close to your father Abba Eugene.
You bore the suffering of a false accusation
To show the Lord fights our battles as we endure to the
    end.

Luke 9:21 to 27, I Corinthians 6:12 to 20

AGATHON OF EGYPT
MARCH 2, 5TH CENTURY

A MONK IS ONE who possesses nothing. He is the possession of God. In a story in the *Sayings of the Desert Fathers*, Abba Macarius the Great was walking up to his cell after gathering grasses for weaving. There he saw a robber taking out his possessions and loading them on a donkey. The monk came, helped the thief take his goods, and praised God for removing material distractions from his life. It is possible that Abba Agathon, a contemporary of Macarius, heard and took this lesson to heart. Like any monk, he owned little or nothing beyond the clothes on his back. However, he did have a little knife that he used for cutting the grasses he needed to weave baskets and brush that may have been in his way.

One day while harvesting wild plants to eat, another monk noticed the knife and complemented Agathon on it. The Abba gladly gave it to the brother as a gift. When asked why, he replied, "I would assume a leper's body and give him mine." This desert father not only spoke of a radical co-suffering. He lived it.

Agathon has thirty lessons attributed to him in the *Sayings of the Desert Fathers,* focused on humility and perseverance in constant prayer. Among these lessons, he said, "Prayer is warfare to the last breath."

MEDITATION

As we engage in spiritual warfare
Remind us of the importance of prayer, Holy Abba
    Agathon,
That we would continue this link to our Father
Until our final breath.

Matthew 6:19 to 24

BISHOP SERAPION OF THMUIS, EGYPT
MARCH 21, 370*

SERAPION PURSUED A LIFE of holiness emulating John the Forerunner, even wearing rough clothing (a sindon). He had no income as to buy food or shelter. Even when others gave him these necessities, he shared or gave them way to others worse off than himself. Serapion found the community of monks in the Sketis Desert of Lower Egypt and lived among them. For a time, he was a disciple of Abba Anthony the Great.

As he struggled against his own passions, Serapion also evangelized to others. He sold himself into slavery to a Greek actor. The monk's righteous example led the master to free him and asked that he would remain with him as a brother. A Greek philosopher was also astonished by Serapion's holy life, as he didn't even take notice of the value of a gold coin that was given to him. He cared more about nourishing souls than his own body or gaining wealth.

His example of compassion, humility, and selflessness led to his being ordained as bishop of Thmuis, a town near the Nile River Delta. While serving there, he became friends with the Patriarch Athanasius the Great. Serapion spent his last years as a simple monk in the desert. There are liturgical texts and lessons in *The Sayings of the Desert Fathers* attributed to him.

(*Prologue of Ohrid dates his death at 358.*)

MEDITATION

An imitator of the life of Holy John the Baptist and
      Forerunner,
Abba Serapion, you denied yourself of gold and luxuries.
Pray to God that we will be blessed with leadership
That will concern themselves with feeding our souls.

Matthew 10:7 to 10, I Corinthians 4:9 to 16

WEEK FOUR

ST. ATHANASIUS

ATHANASIUS THE GREAT

MAY 2, 373

THIS EGYPTIAN NATIVE served the Church in times of major transitions. He saw the end of an era of widespread persecutions when Emperor Constantine's Edict of Milan in 313 made Christianity one of the legal religions in the Roman Empire. As congregations became more common throughout the empire, the priest Arius began teaching that Jesus was not consubstantial or coeternal with God the Father. Arius' false doctrine became so widespread that the entire Church had to get together and decide what to do about it. The First Ecumenical Council came together in Nicaea in 325. Deacon Athanasius helped produce the First Nicaean Creed which declared Jesus to be "eternally begotten of the Father," and "true God of true God, of one essence with the Father."

Despite being proven wrong, Arius and his followers persuaded later emperors to exile Athanasius on several occasions after Athanasius had risen to become the Bishop of Alexandria. During one period of exile, he spent time in the Egyptian deserts and met monks who renounced the world for a more intensive struggle against their passions and sins. This led the bishop to write *The Life of St. Anthony the Great*. This book encouraged the growth of Christian monasticism worldwide.

After returning to the bishopric seat, he put together a list of books that would be good for the clergy of Africa to use for teaching and preaching. This list of 27 books became very popular among clergy and laity from all over the known world. Eventually, this list would be canonized in the Council of Carthage in 398 as the New Testament. Athanasius himself reposed on May 2nd, 373. He and his later successor, Cyril, are celebrated as "Pillars of the Faith" with a feast day on January 18th.

MEDITATION

Solid pillar of the truth standing against all falsehood,
Brother to the poor righteous ones of the desert,
Reveal the ancient faith to your children of the diaspora,
    Athanasius.
May the Lord strengthen me to stand as you did, Holy
    Father.

John 1:1-14, 2 Timothy 4:1-5

CYRIL, ARCHBISHOP OF ALEXANDRIA

JUNE 9, 444

DESPITE THE DECISIONS made in the First Ecumenical Council, the Church still struggled against false doctrines being taught by misleading teachers. Another wise Patriarch of Alexandria and Africa would be called upon to defend the truth. Cyril was born and educated in the city, gaining a reputation for intelligence and wisdom. In 412, he was selected to succeed his uncle, Patriarch Theophilus. Despite the Roman Empire now patronizing Christianity, there were various conflicts with Jews and pagans. With advice and prayers of the Desert Fathers, Cyril led his flock effectively.

Another danger came from the Patriarch of Constantinople, Nestorius of Syria. He taught that Christ was two separate sons, one human and the other divine. Also, he refused to call the Virgin Mary the "Theotokos" (bearer of God), instead referring to her as the "Christotokos" (bearer of Christ). A Third Ecumenical Council was called in 431 to settle the matter. Through careful and wise discussion, it was found that Jesus Christ was both fully human and fully divine, two distinct natures in One Incarnate Being. As Jesus was God Incarnate, Mary did bear God and should be acknowledged as the Theotokos.

Not everyone will be pleased with the truth. We are called to stand on it and to explain it like Cyril with the prayers of the Church.

MEDITATION

Solid pillar of the truth standing against all falsehood,
Devotee of the Mother of God,
Reveal the ancient faith to your children of the diaspora,
    Cyril.
May the Lord strengthen me to stand as you did, Holy
    Father.

Luke 1:34, 35, 39-45, 48

MEDITATION FOR ATHANASIUS AND CYRIL

Athanasius & Cyril; Two strong arms of truth,
Two powerful legs of righteousness,
Help us to hold on to and stand on the rock of our
    salvation,
Jesus Christ our Lord.

ZACHARIAS THE RECLUSE OF EGYPT
MARCH 24

A RECLUSE LIVES ALONE and avoids contact with others. By definition, many of the Desert Fathers and most other hermits could have "recluse" added to their names. The advantage of being a recluse is that one has less time to think about and judge the actions of others. Instead, the recluse is likely to ponder his own shortcomings and be repentant.

Zacharias lived alone. However, even in his solitude he had a mind for homeless and poor people. He followed the example of the scriptures in practicing the virtues of aiding those in need. Consideration for the state of one's soul is important, but it cannot bear fruit without the love of one's neighbor as oneself. The life of this recluse reminds us to be compassionate to those less fortunate, for he cared so much for the poor that he became known as a patron saint of people who are homeless and outcast.

MEDITATION

Living alone did not mean you cared for no one else.
Indeed, your great love poured out to those around you,
Abba Zacharias the Reclusive one.
May God grant us a loving presence beyond empty
    words.

Luke 6:20, 21, Acts 2:44, 45, James 2:1 to 9

PAPHNUTIUS

APRIL 19, 4TH CENTURY

PAPHNUTIUS WAS FROM the Upper Thebaid and was a "passion bearer," one who suffered great persecution for the faith. Under the Roman Emperor Maximius, he was badly tortured, blinded in one eye, and sentenced to work in a mine. Released from imprisonment, Paphnutius became a monastic disciple of Abba Anthony the Great. Seeing the threat of the Arian heresy, he joined Athanasius the Great at Nicaea for the First Ecumenical Council in 325.

Emperor Constantine was very moved when he saw Paphnutius because of the wounds he suffered during the persecutions. Although a strict celibate himself, the monk advised the council of the ancient tradition of the Church. Unmarried clergy should remain as such. Unmarried men must choose to be married or remain celibate before being ordained.

Paphnutius recorded the *Histories of the Monks of Upper Egypt,* which tells how he and other desert dwellers of the region brought Christianity to ancient Nubia. He was the abbot of four monasteries and has six lessons in the Sayings of the Desert Fathers attributed to him.

MEDITATION

Though beaten and cast down,
Truth and wisdom arise throughout the world.
Abba Paphnutius, pray to God for correct instruction
For all believers and those who will receive the Gospel.

Matthew 7:1 to 5, I Corinthians 7:1 to 9,
I Timothy 3:1 to 12

PACHOMIUS THE GREAT
348

ABBA ANTHONY BECAME the symbol of the desert hermits. Macarius developed the "Sketis Way" with monks in proximity to one another with the freedom to develop their individual rules. Pachomius became the founder of the cenobitic (community) way, with monks living together and following a shared rule in the monastery.

The saint was born in the Thebaid region of Egypt in a pagan family. After serving in the Roman Army, he converted to Christianity. He began monastic life under the guidance of Palamon in Upper Egypt. After a number of years, Pachomius was guided by the Lord to build a monastery on the ruins of a village called Tabennisi. Other monks sought to emulate his model of labor and prayer. They also respected how he overcame many temptations. Pachomius gave a single rule for all that would follow him. The monks followed a common diet, times of prayer, and assigned tasks for the good of the community.

Due to the strictness of the monastery rule, Pachomius could not even see his sister, Maria, who came to visit him. However, he did bless and instruct her to build a hut not far from the monastery. Eventually, women monastics came to her to direct them establishing a monastery for nuns.

About seven thousand monks came to live in the monasteries built by Pachomius. Yet, he remained humble. He had a reputation for being strict with himself and compassionate to others. He visited ill monks and loosened fasting restrictions on them to help them recover. Pachomius himself became ill and died in his fifties. Abba Theodore, his close disciple, was his successor.

MEDITATION

Abba Pachomius, God gave you the vision of fraternal
    spirit
Of men and women living fully devoted to prayer.
Pray to God that we may see the holiness in each other
And may grow together as the body of Christ.

Matthew 23:1 12

†HEODORE THE SANCTIFIED
MAY 16, 368

THEODORE WAS RAISED in a wealthy Christian home in Upper Egypt. He loved the monastic ideal and ran away from home at the age of fourteen, seeking to enter one of the monasteries of Tabennisi. Led by God, the teenager found and was well received by Pachomius the Great. Theodore was very obedient to the monastery rule. He even refused to see his mother even when ordered to do so by the bishop. He was intelligent enough to be trusted to teach the scriptures to the other monks. Many of the brothers grumbled at this since he was only in his twenties. Yet the spirit of God was upon him, and Abbot Pachomius saw his potential.

Theodore was the first of the monks with Abbot Pachomius to be ordained into the priesthood. Thus, the Church calls him, 'the Sanctified.' As Pachomius began to withdraw more as a hermit, Theodore was given more supervisory task at the Tabennisi monastery. He constantly looked after the Abbot as he was dying of his illness. When Pachomius reposed, Theodore was given charge over all of the monasteries in the Thebaid region. During this time, he developed a reputation for working miracles as well as for his holy living, even attracting the attention of the Patriarch Athanasius. When Abba Theodore reposed in 368, it is said that monks on the opposite side of the Nile could hear the sound of mourning coming from Tabennisi.

MEDITATION
Even as a youth, you relentlessly pursued the path to
   holiness.
Yielding to the great abbas of the Thebaid,
Sanctified Theodore grew into a father among fathers.
May a portion of your spirit continue to fall on us
   children.

John 8:54 to 58, I Timothy 4:12 to 5:2

BESSARION THE GREAT
466

BESSARION, A NATIVE EGYPTIAN, sought to live in holiness from his youth. After baptism, he began to practice strict asceticism and journeyed to the Holy Land to learn from the monastics there. He returned to Egypt and became a monk under Abba Isadore. Bessarion's monastic discipline went beyond that of most of his contemporaries. He would go without food for forty days at a time. Once he remained motionless during one of those fasts. His focus was on prayer and being one with God.

Through his concentrated spiritual life, the Lord worked miracles by Bessarion's prayers. He was able to make foul water fresh to drink. Rain fell on the land as he prayed during a drought. Because he spent most of his life in silence, he did not boast about an ability to do these things.

Despite his discipline and wonderworking, Bessarion was a very humble man, not considering himself to be any better than any other person. In *The Sayings of the Desert Fathers*, a priest called for a man to be removed from a Divine Liturgy because he had fallen into sin. As the man left, Bessarion went with him. Someone asked, "Abba, why are you leaving the service?" "Because I am a sinner too," he replied. Eleven other lessons of this Desert Father are included in the afore mentioned book.

MEDITATION
Humble Bessarion, you lived the holy and monastic way,
Yet when a sinner was cast out of church you also went
away.
Do not forsake us who have fallen to temptation,
But walk with and show us the way to Christ our Lord
and God.

Matthew 7:13, 14, Titus 2:6 to 8

WEEK FIVE

ST. MOSES THE BLACK

MOSES THE BLACK
AUGUST 28, 375

MOSES WAS A VERY DARK-skinned (Ethiopian=burnt face) former slave and bandit near Alexandria. When he was attempting to rob a monastery in the Sketis Desert, the monks led by Abba Isadore warmly welcomed him. Moses, moved by this reception, converted to the faith and became a monk. He struggled for over a decade with temptations of his former life. Abba Isadore encouraged him that becoming holy takes time.

Over the years, Moses was a great example of compassion and forgiveness. A number of monks wanted him to become a priest. The Patriarch of Alexandria and other clergy tested him by ridiculing his black skin. When they saw that he blamed himself rather than retaliate or lose heart, he was ordained to the priesthood. This was not a demonstration that it was right to mock skin color, but a demonstration of Moses' extreme humility.

One of the brothers was caught in sin, and Moses was asked to serve on a sentencing council. After refusing initially, he came to the council carrying a bag of sand with a leak. As he came to the brothers, they asked why he carried such a thing. "The sand leaks from the bag behind me, and I don't see it anymore. And you ask me to judge my brother?" This was to demonstrate that no one knows the extent of their own sinfulness, and therefore no one can truly judge another person righteously. (A slightly different version of this story, with Moses carrying a leaking jug of water, is related in *The Sayings of the Desert Fathers*.)

A band of Vandals killed Moses and seven other monks who attempted to show them the same hospitality he received at a monastery years before.

MEDITATION

Tested on the color of his skin
Abba Moses won over brothers by his purity of heart.
Pray to God that we see beyond what is superficial
And patiently grow in His grace and mercy.

Matthew 7:1-5

PAISIUS THE GREAT

JUNE 19, 400

PAISIUS WAS BORN to Christian parents who were known for their generosity. When his father died, an angel of God led his mother to let the boy be raised by the clergy, after the examples of the Prophet Samuel and Mary the Theotokos, who had been brought up by priests.

Paisius began his monastic life under the guidance of Abba Pambo and fully embraced his assigned labors and instruction. He constantly read spiritual books, fasted, and prayed. The monk is said to have fasted for 70 days after taking the Eucharist.

He later went to the Nitrian Desert, where he dug a cell for himself with his hands. In a vision, the Lord told him that a monastery would arise there with many other monks. This was fulfilled in time as monks and laymen willingly obeyed the rule established by Abba Paisius. Instead of following their own desires, these disciples sought to do the will of the elders.

One monk took it upon himself to move closer to the city, where he had relations with an unbelieving woman. She tempted him to leave the faith. Some of the brothers from Nitria came to see him. Seeing how far he had fallen, he asked the monks to ask Paisius to pray for him. Paisius did so, and afterward the unbelieving woman companion died. The man returned to the monastery and came back to Abba Paisius, deeply repenting having left.

Paisius lived in a cave further away from the monastery to maintain his peace. His example of disciplined spiritual living and mercy to the repentant was a beacon for others to live by.

MEDITATION

Prayer, work, and spiritual reading were cornerstones of
your life in Christ.
Paisius, let us carefully learn from your ways
That we will not reject and condemn our fallen brothers
and sisters,
But embrace them as they return to God in repentance.

Luke 15:11 to 32, Galatians 6:1 to 5

SISOES THE GREAT

JULY 6, 429

SISOES WAS BORN in Thebes. He began his monastic journey in the Sketis Desert under the guidance of Abba Or. Like some other Desert Fathers, he left to seek a deeper spiritual life as a hermit. Sisoes was very strict in his asceticism. At times, his disciple Abraham had to remind him when to stop fasting and eat. One of his great struggles was against anger. With much prayer and effort, he gained an unshakeable peace in mind.

Despite being harsh with himself, Sisoes was very compassionate and forgiving to others. In the *Sayings of the Desert Fathers*, another monk came to him among the brothers seeking to do three years of penance for a grave sin. "That's a bit much," said the elder. "Should I do three months?" "That's still much." Other monks chimed in, "What about three weeks?" Sisoes advised, "If he has sincerely repented and does not intend to fall again, I say three days is sufficient."

In his sixty years of spiritual discipline, the Lord blessed him to perform miracles. Once he brought a child back from the dead. Yet he remained humble, considering himself inferior to his contemporaries. On his deathbed, Sisoes begged that God would give him more time to repent. The monks around him said, "Abba, you have no need to repent." The elder replied, "I don't think that I've even begun to repent." Fifty-four lessons in *The Sayings of the Desert Fathers* are attributed to him.

Pharisees of old put heavy burdens on the backs of men;
In wisdom great Sisoes saw the harshness of extreme
  penances.
Humility and sincerity are what the repentant shall offer
  unto God.
Teach us to walk always in these ways.

Mark 1:14

SARAH OF THE NILE
JULY 13, 370

SARAH IS ONE of a few women with lessons found in *The Sayings of the Desert Fathers*. The same sayings are included in the *Matericon*, a collection addressed to nuns and translated by the Russian monastic Theophan the Recluse in the 19th century.

Sarah was still a young virgin when she came to live in a desert near the Nile River. Yet, to avoid vanity, she never took the time to see her face in its waters. As with any young monastic, she struggled against lustful thoughts for many years. But she never asked that the Lord would take these temptations from her. She simply prayed, "Lord, give me strength." After over a decade of struggle, the demon of lust left. It appeared to her and said, "Sarah, you have defeated me." "No, it's the Lord Jesus who defeated you," she replied.

Two monks sought to mock the Amma. Arriving at her cell, they said, "Be careful not to boast in your heart that two monks have come to see me, a woman." "Yes, I am a woman by nature," she replied, "But, not by worth." By this, she was not putting down women but putting to shame their low estimation of the worth of women, for she was better at imitating Christ's virtues than they.

Over the years, more women were drawn to monasticism with Sarah as model for living. She advised inquirers to struggle against their chief temptation, and the other temptations would fall as well. For her, silence and stillness were essential in spiritual living.

MEDITATION

Mother Sarah, pray to God to give us strength in our
    struggles.
Lust and vanity surround us to stir up our souls to sin,
Yet by silence and stillness we can overcome our enemy.
Guide us in this way of Christ that our souls may be
    saved.

Luke 1:1-3, Galatians 3:28, Titus 2:3-5

PAMBO

JULY 18, 386

PAMBO LIVED IN the Nitrian Desert of Lower Egypt. As with other desert dwelling ascetics, people came to him seeking spiritual advice. The monk refrained from answering too quickly. He told inquirers that he needed time to think and pray before receiving an answer from God.

Pambo ate from what he earned by his own labor. It was said that he worked to the point of exhaustion. Saint Melania the Younger came to him with much silver for the needs of his monastery. It took constant pleading from her for the Abbot Pambo to receive the gift and have it distributed.

Other notable early Christians held Pambo in high regard. Abba Anthony himself said that Pambo's fear of God caused the Holy Spirit to dwell in him. His humility drew people to him. Theophilus, Patriarch of Alexandria, was visiting the monks and saw Pambo. The brothers urged the old man to share a word of salvation with the highest clergyman of Africa. He replied, "If my silence is not helpful to him, of what use are my words?" Fourteen lessons in *The Sayings of the Desert Fathers* are attributed to Him.

MEDITATION

Wisely, Abba Pambo avoided speaking too quickly or
    often,
Preferring the presence of God to share through silence.
Let us not chase after the wealth of this world, but
May the Lord bless the humble work of our hands.

Matthew 25:31-45

POEMEN THE SHEPHERD
AUGUST 27, 450

As A BOY, POEMEN visited Abba Paisius the Great. The elder said, "One day he will save others, and the hand of God is with him." Years later, he and his two brothers became monks. Their mother missed them greatly and came to the monastery hoping to see them. Poemen came as far as the gate and asked, "Where would you rather see us, in this world or the world to come?" She left the gate with the joyful expectation of seeing her offspring in heaven.

He and his brother, Abba Anoub, were known for their challenging ascetic practices, such as eating no more than one meal a day and getting four hours of sleep. The rest of their day was filled with work and prayer. Yet, Poemen was compassionate on those who struggled with sins and temptations. Like Abba Sisoes, he taught that God was merciful to one who did an earnest and sincere penance for a few days rather than a lengthy self-imposed punishment.

Poemen guided the monks around him as a shepherd more than a taskmaster. A brother came to him and asked if he should lead a group that wanted to be his disciples. The Abba advised, "Live as you should, and they will decide whether or not to follow you. Be the example, not the legislator" (*The Sayings of the Desert Fathers*).

MEDITATION

Not by force or threat did you lead others to holy
    wisdom.
Abba Poemen, you were a model and a shepherd.
Show us the way of asceticism and mercy,
Keeping our hope on obtaining a heavenly home.

Mark 8:34-38, I Corinthians 11:1

†HEODORA OF ALEXANDRIA
SEPTEMBER 11, 490

WHEN SHE WAS A MARRIED YOUNG woman, another man sought to seduce Theodora into adultery with him. She refused him for quite some time, until he hired another woman to convince her that God does not see the sins committed in darkness. Misled by false wisdom, she betrayed her husband.

Realizing her error, Theodora cut off her hair in anguish. She fled her home to find a place to live in repentance. Rather than a women's monastery where her husband would likely find her, she disguised herself as a man and sought entry to a men's monastery. The abbot tested the stranger's sincerity by having him (her) spend the night outside of the monastery gates. The abbot and other monks knew her as the monk Theodore. She grew in God's grace through her deep repentance and ascetic discipline.

As with Mary of Alexandria, Theodora was wrongfully accused of impregnating a young woman who tried and failed to seduce the monk into sin. The abbot drove Theodore out of the monastery, where he raised the child. After years of banishment, he was allowed back into the brotherhood and continued to instruct the boy. When the monk died, it was revealed that he was really Theodora. The monks found and brought her husband to the monastery, where he also

92

became a monk. The son whom she instructed, in time, became the abbot.

Theodora is included in *The Sayings of the Desert Fathers* with ten lessons attributed to her. This was likely also the same noble nun who received instruction from Abba Isaiah (a disciple of Abba Macarius the Great) in the *Matericon*, a collection of monastic wisdom featuring Desert Mothers.

MEDITATION
Misled into sin, you proved to be a model of repentance
And bore the cost of false accusation.
Abbess Theodora, pray for us
That we will also receive Godly grace and wisdom.

Luke 12:11-12

WEEK SIX

ST. MARY OF EGYPT

MARY OF EGYPT

APRIL 1, 421

THIS IS ONE of the most well-loved stories of redemption in Orthodoxy. Mary became promiscuous as a young teenager in Alexandria, sometimes not accepting money for her encounters. One day, she saw a group of men taking a ship to Jerusalem to venerate the Holy Cross. She joined them, using her body to pay for her passage there. Arriving in Jerusalem, she tried to make her way into the church, but an invisible force blocked her attempts. At that point, she realized that she couldn't enter because of her sinful lifestyle. With tears of repentance, she prayed before an icon of the Theotokos, promising that if she were allowed to enter, she would pursue a different way of life.

With her prayer answered, Mary made good on her promise. She took a boat across the Jordan River and lived in the desert alone. For fourteen years she struggled against her lust as well as desires for fine food and wine. After some forty years being exposed to the elements, her clothing wore completely off, leaving her naked. When Mary had spent about forty-seven years in the desert, seeing no other human or beast, Abba Zosimas found her as he journeyed fasting during Great Lent. Mary asked the monk to throw her his monastic cloak and then to provide her with the Eucharist the next year, with the promise that he would see her again during the following Lenten Fast. He communed her the following year and made a plan to return the next year to the same spot to meet her. That year, she reposed, and a lion helped bury the saint. Her story is a part of the Canon of St. Andrew of Crete, and she is venerated on the Fifth Sunday of Great Lent.

MEDITATION

Sin had scarred your body and soul,
Yet you shed tears and lived in repentance.
Holy Mary of Egypt, pray to God for us
That we would also change direction to walk in holiness.

Luke 3:1-9, John 8:2-11

EUPHROSYNE & PAPHNUTIUS
5TH CENTURY

AN ABBOT WAS ASKED by an elderly couple to pray that they might bear a child. By God's grace, Euphrosyne was born. Unfortunately, her mother died while she was very young. Her father, Paphnutius, was very wealthy and gave his daughter the best of everything. However, she saw greater riches in the kingdom of heaven and wished to commit herself to celibacy for life. When her father sought to marry her off to a wealthy young man, she fled to a men's monastery. Disguised as a man, she became known as the monk Smaragdus. Her abbot, the same one who prayed for her birth, gave her instruction, and she made great progress in spiritual living.

Sorrowful over the loss of his daughter, Paphnutius sought consolation from the abbot. Smaragdus was given charge of the grieving father, who did not recognize the monk's identity. Smaragdus taught the old man to sell his material goods and distribute all to the poor. Appreciating his wisdom, Paphnutius continued to see this monk often.

When Smaragdus became ill, Paphnutius realized it was Euphrosyne speaking to him all the time. When she died, her father sold all of his possessions and became a monk. He lived in her cell until he reposed years later.

MEDITATION

As a child, you desired more than material things
And advised your own father of this great wisdom.
Euphrosyne, help us put aside the shallow pursuits of life
And grow in and share with others the wonders of God.

Matthew 19:11-12, Mark 8:35-37

AMMON

OCTOBER 4, 350

AMUN (AMMON OR AMOUN) was the name of the ancient Egyptian god of the air. Worship of him was combined with that of the sun god, Ra. Amun-Ra was one of the most widely venerated deities over a thousand years before Christ. In the fourth century, a notable Christian monastic would also bear this name.

Ammon was a young man forced into marriage. Not wanting to break his commitment to living a celibate lifestyle, he encouraged his bride to live with him as brother and sister instead of as a married couple. They did so for almost 20 years. His wife remained in their home and established it as a convent with other nuns. Ammon moved to the Desert of Nitria and became a hermit. It is said by some that he established the monastic community at Kellia.

Ammon was an example of humility. Once, a hermit new to the desert came to his cell and asked if there was a small hut nearby where he could live and pray. "I'll go and see, stay here," Ammon replied. The elder went and built a cell and began to live in it. Days had passed when the hermit realized that his host had given him his cell with everything in it. Three lessons from *The Sayings of the Desert Fathers* are attributed to Amoun (Ammon) of Nitria.

MEDITATION

Though named for a pagan deity
Abba Ammon lived and taught the way of the Holy
    Trinity.
Sacrificing even the honorable state of matrimony,
His desert life is a beacon for us to follow God.

Matthew 5:41-42, Luke 3:10-11

✝THAIS

(TAISIA)

OCTOBER 8, 340

TWO SAINTS NAMED THAIS are on the Orthodox Christian calendar. Long before becoming a nun, Thais was raised in a home far from godly living. Men throughout Egypt sought her out for her beauty. Abba Paphnutius sought her out for salvation. Dressed in worldly clothing, the monk came to her with a gold coin, and she led him to a private place. Thinking he wanted a sexual favor from her, she closed and locked the door.

Instead, Paphnutius sternly rebuked her lifestyle and warned her to repent while she still had time. Cut to the heart, Thais threw away her profits from prostitution and lived in a cell for three years in tears of repentance. She constantly prayed, "My Creator, have mercy on me!" The abba comforted her that God saw her tears and forgave her sins. She reposed three days afterwards. Abba Paul the Simple saw a vision of a place in heaven prepared for the repentant woman.

MEDITATION

God does not wish to destroy depraved sinners
But to bring all to salvation.

Blessed Thais, the Lord did not leave you in the midst of
    wickedness
You took His hand and found deliverance for your soul.

Luke 7:36-50, 15:3-10

✝HAIS

SHE WAS AN ORPHAN of wealthy and pious parents. As a young woman, she was known for being a generous almsgiver. When her money was spent, she gave in to the temptation of selling her body. Some of the monks in the Sketis Desert heard of her situation and resolved to help her.

Abba John the Dwarf came to her house. Thais allowed him in, thinking that he was some random monk who had found some valuable gems. Seated with her, the elder began to weep, "You have betrayed Jesus Christ, your bridegroom, and have surrendered to wicked deeds."

His words cut her to the heart. However, Abba John comforted her saying, "The Lord comes to rescue those who have strayed. If you repent, He will take you back as His bride." She immediately followed the elder out of her house without saying a word to her servants. Night fell as they went into the desert. He prepared a place for Thais to sleep while he went a short distance away to pray and sleep.

Abba John was awakened around midnight by a bright light from the sky to where she was sleeping. He saw angels lift up her soul and take it to heaven. When it disappeared, he saw that Thais was dead. An angel comforted him saying, "Because she repented with all of her soul and sincere heart, her hour of repentance was equal to many years." (Quotations here are drawn from *The Sayings of the Desert Fathers*.)

MEDITATION

Tears of repentance wash away the deepest stains of sin. Blessed Thais, you have shown us this truth. Your heartfelt tears reached from the desert into heaven And lifted you into the arms of the Lord.

Luke 7:36-50, 15:21-27

ISADORA OF †ABENNISI
MAY 10, 365

SOME ORTHODOX SAINTS lived so virtuously that they feared that people would honor them, which honor would give occasion to the devil to fill their heads with pride and conceit. Thus, they would act as if they were mentally ill or simpleminded so that no one would think too highly of them. Such men and women were called "Fools for Christ."

Isadora was an Egyptian nun who sought to be the lowliest person in her convent. Her clothing was mere rags. She did the work other sisters avoided and ate their leftover food after she served them. Her peers mocked and ridiculed her, because she seemed to be insane. Some even cursed and slapped her.

Abba Pitirim had a vision from God that he should honor the wise nun who lived in the convent for her holy living. The Abbess welcomed him in and he met all of the sisters. However, he did not see the one to honor. When he was introduced to Isadora, the monk immediately fell to her feet and blessed her. "But Abba, she is insane," the sisters said. "You are the insane ones. May God grant me half of the reward in store for her in heaven." Ashamed of the way they thought of and treated her, the abbess and sisters repented and honored the once scorned sister. Fearing receiving rewards in this life over the

106

next, Isadora fled to a far-off monastery, where she later reposed.

MEDITATION

Cursed and insulted as you accepted the bottom rung of
    the ladder,
Faithful Isadora, you proved not to be a fool among
    sisters.
Teach us to embrace humility and even bear insult
And not wallow in the praises of this world.

Matthew 11:25-30, I Corinthians 1:20-25

JOHN THE DWARF

NOVEMBER 9, 407

ALTHOUGH NOT GREAT in stature, Abba John the Dwarf was a giant among the Desert Fathers. Two stories from *The Sayings of the Desert Fathers* reveal how he grew in the disciplines of labor and obedience.

Having a zeal for the spiritual life, John told his older brother, "I will stop working and go to the desert to live among the angels." After a few days, John realized how cold it could get at night without some sort of shelter or covering. He became very hungry not long afterward. After walking back a long distance, he knocked on his brother's door. "It is I, John, your brother." "Impossible," replied the elder. "My brother has no need of anything. He lives in the desert like an angel and doesn't work." After hearing this rebuke, John stayed on his brother's doorstep until morning. As his brother let him inside, John repented and began working.

As directed by an abba in the Sketis Desert, John planted a dry stick in the desert sand and watered it each day for three years. He had to walk a great distance each evening and morning to reach the water. Nevertheless, he did this faithfully until the third year, when the stick grew small branches with leaves and fruit. He and his abba took some of the fruit to the church, where the abba told the brothers, "This is the fruit of obedience."

A Roman aristocrat, Arsenius, found John the Dwarf and became his disciple before becoming a noted hermit in his own right. Other monks asked this abba to visit Thais and lead her away from prostitution. Forty-seven lessons from *The Sayings of the Desert Fathers* are attributed to him, including the quotes excerpted here.

MEDITATION
Lacking in human stature, you are a giant among the
    saints.
Abba John, you stand tall in obedience and wisdom.
Pray to God that we learn your ways of labor and prayer
And prove a worthy model of life for our brothers and
    sisters.

Luke 19:1-10, 2 Thessalonians 3:1-15

WEEK SEVEN

ST. AUGUSTINE

AUGUSTINE OF HIPPO
430

ALL CHRISTIANS STRUGGLE with sin. Even the greatest of saints had very strong temptations to deal with at times. Before becoming a prominent leader in the Church, Augustine struggled greatly with mental and physical fornication, as did many young men. He studied in Carthage and became a noted teacher of rhetoric. During those years, he practiced the Persian religion, Manichaeism, and later, Platonism. But he couldn't find the access to Truth that he craved in either place. He felt moved toward the Christian faith but couldn't understand how such simple, unsophisticated scriptures could hold wisdom.

Through the prayers of his pious mother, Monica, he moved to Italy where Ambrose of Milan led and converted him to the Christian faith in 387. Ambrose showed Augustine how to read spiritually, with Christ as the key to the meaning of the Bible. Augustine described his conversion in many of his works. In one of them, he said that the Truth that he could see on a far, unreachable shore was finally reachable when he clung to the Cross of Christ, on which he could sail to Truth as on a boat. Renouncing his former ways, Augustine returned to Africa and established a small monastic community. He was ordained to the priesthood and bishop of the city of Hippo in 396.

One of the false teachings he taught against was Pelagianism, the belief that it was possible for people to find salvation simply by being a good person. Augustine wrote many arguments against this and every other false teaching of his day that denied the need for the mercy and grace of God in Christ. He is best known for his teachings on discernment of the grace and love of God, both in regular human lives and throughout history. His view of "original sin" as a tendency toward sin which people pass along because of the social nature of sin has often been misunderstood because of the way it was interpreted by later writers. Even so, we are moved by the honesty of his struggle with sin and his profound experience of the mercy of God in his *Confessions*, his recognition of the image of the Triune God in humans and demonstration that the Triune God created the whole Creation in his *On the Trinity*, and his elaboration of God's revelation of Christ in all of history and the coming reign of God in *The City of God*.

MEDITATION

Blessed Augustine, we are also wounded by so many
    temptations and sins.
When you poured out your soul to the Lord, He healed
    and strengthened you in struggles.
Do not forget your children of the diaspora and all
    believers.
Pray to the Lord that He will cleanse us as we confess to
    Him.

John 8:1-11, Romans 7:21-25

MONICA OF AFRICA
MAY 4, 387

WE ARE TOLD to "Train up a child in the way he should go. And when he is old, he will not depart from it." Monica, the pious Christian wife of a pagan African official tried to do this with her three children even though her husband did not allow them to be baptized. Augustine gave her the most grief, as he had a child with a concubine. Seeing her constant and tearful prayers, her husband was won over to the Christian faith before his repose.

While studying and teaching rhetoric in Carthage, Augustine joined the Manichaean religion. She sought the help of a former Manichean clergyman to help persuade him away from the sect. He would not try to reason with him. For almost a decade, she prayed with the hope that God would answer her. In 383, Monica went with Augustine as he lectured in Rome and Milan. After meeting and listening to Bishop Ambrose, the rhetorician abandoned his false belief and was baptized into the Church four years later. St. Ambrose said that her tears for Augustine were what led to Augustine's salvation. Monica followed a different pattern of worship in Carthage and Africa than she found in Italy. Not knowing what to make of this, Ambrose instructed her, "When in Rome, do as the Romans do."

Augustine and Monica were on their way back to Africa when she died at the port city of Ostia after an experience of profound peace and joint prayer together. From her life, we learn to be patient with our wayward friends and family and constantly pray for them. Also, we are encouraged by her example to accept different cultural norms, as long as the Church teaches the true doctrine.

MEDITATION

With great patience, you remained in union with an
    unbelieving husband.
With great patience, you watched a son live waywardly.
But the joy of the Lord fell upon you, O Monica
Through patience, your son joined the ranks of the great
    Saints.

Romans 13:12-14, I Corinthians 7:12-14,

PATAPIUS

DECEMBER 8, 463

PATAPIUS WAS BORN in the Upper Egyptian city of Thebes in a prominent Christian home. Despite learning a wealth of secular knowledge, he was very interested in living as an ascetic in a desert. He did so after his father died, and a great fame about him spread throughout Egypt.

Wishing not to be disturbed from his life of prayer, he made his way to Constantinople. No one except a fellow Egyptian disciple knew him. Patapius was granted a cell at the Blachernae Monastery, where he continued in prayer and silence.

After a short time, people came to him for prayer, as God gave him wonderworking power. Sometimes ill and infirm people lined up outside of his cell seeking a blessing from him. Rather than trying to flee to another place to hide, Patapius remained at the monastery, making sure not to change from his simple way of spiritual living. He reposed in his eighties and was buried at the Church of St. John the Baptist.

MEDITATION

Our Savior taught that a lamp cannot be hidden under a basket.

You bright light of faith could not be hidden in Africa or Europe.

Abba Patapius, pray to God that we may always work in humility

And simply cooperate with Him to work with us.

Matthew 5:14-16, Luke 8:16-18

ISAAC OF FAYOUM
MAY 20, 356

LIKE SOME OTHER SAINTS, Isaac sought the monastic life from a young age. He resided in the oasis-rich area of Fayoum in a cave on Mount El-Sharika. Led by an angel, Abba Anthony came to the mountain and instructed Isaac and a group of believers living as monks.

Isaac was a healer and spiritual father to ten former pagans who were committed to monasticism. They built the St. Mary El-Hammam Monastery in 346, which still has a community of monks to this day. Patriarch Peter II of Alexandria ordained Abba Isaac to the priesthood. He gave care and instruction to monastics in the Mount El-Khazain region until his repose in 356.

This is not the Isaac (Priest of the Cells) whose works are in *The Sayings of the Desert Fathers*. That other Isaac was a hermit in the Nitria Desert and the successor to Abba Cronius, but he was eventually exiled for heresy. Isaac of Fayoum who taught the converts and established the monastery that still nurtures a community of monks today kept the faith soundly as he received it.

MEDITATION

Let us not overlook and ignore the unbeliever,
As Abba Isaac led such to the glories of God in the desert.
God continues to bless this legacy to our time
For His mercy does endure forever.

Matthew 6:25-34, II Timothy 2:1-10

ISIDORE OF PELUSIA

FEBRUARY 4, 436

THIS ISIDORE WAS born and raised in Alexandria in a very pious family, related to both Cyril and Theophilus, who served as Archbishops. Rather than pursuing ministry in the city, he fled to Mt. Pelusium and lived in asceticism. His education in sacred and secular matters helped him become a leader among monastics in the area.

As a priest, Isidore was a noteworthy preacher and gave instruction to ordinary laypersons as well as dignitaries. He supported John Chrysostom during his time of persecution. He also pushed for a Third Ecumenical Council standing against the Nestorian teaching of Christ being two separate persons.

Six of his lessons are included in *The Sayings of the Desert Fathers*.

MEDITATION

Fleeing to the desert, God's truth still radiated from you,
Teaching all men great and small, blessed Isadore.
Pray to God for us in these times of trials
That we will not waver from the true faith.

Matthew 10: 37-42

ISIDORE OF SKETIS
MARCH 13, 4TH CENTURY

THIS MAY BE THE Isidore the Priest with ten lessons in *The Sayings of the Desert Fathers* attributed to him. Saint John Cassian mentions him among the leaders of the Sketis monks. He was the spiritual father to the former bandit, Abba Moses the Black. Once, the elder took him to a mountaintop before sunrise. As dawn's light grew, Isadore taught Moses that one does not become a perfect contemplative in an instant. It takes time for the light to grow in a man.

According to *The Sayings of the Desert Fathers*, Isidore said, "If you desire salvation, do everything that leads you to it." Let us keep this slow and steady focus as we come to the end of Lent, which is only the beginning of our struggle for salvation.

MEDITATION

As you welcomed Moses the Bandit
And guided him to be a holy saint,
Abba Isadore, pray to God for us
To show compassion to those who struggle and seek to
    grow.

Luke 9:23, Galatians 2:20

ONUPHRIUS THE GREAT
JUNE 12, 400

ABBA PAPHNUTIUS WAS LED to the Thebaid Desert to find someone struggling against the passions that he could learn from. There he found Onuphrius, who had lived isolated from human contact for sixty years. The very sight of him was shocking, as his hair had grown so much that it covered his naked body.

Onuphrius had once lived in a Thebaid monastery and followed a rule with other monks. The brothers lived in good harmony with each other in pursuit of heavenly virtues. But he heard his elders speak of how powerful of a prophet Elijah the Tishbite was and how there was no man born of a woman more holy than John the Baptist. Onuphrius left the monastery to try to imitate the way they lived.

He suffered great hunger and thirst. But the hermit was driven to remain alone in the desert, praying and fasting. The Lord rewarded his extreme efforts with food sent to him from the angels and palm fruit. The angels even gave Onuphrius the Eucharist.

Abba Paphnutius was there when the hermit reposed. A bright light shone around him with the sound of angels singing. He told the story of Onuphrius to other monastics to inspire them to seek an angelic lifestyle no matter where they may be.

MEDITATION

In the depths of Egypt your bright light shines for us.
Abba Onuphrius is a model of the Lord's providence.
Stripped of every worldly possession, he was sustained
  as a prophet of old:
He was fed and clothed on the word of God.

Matthew 3:1-6, 11:11

BIBLIOGRAPHY

Prologue of Ohrid Vols I & II, Saint Nikolai Velimirovich, Sebastian Press/Serbian Archdiocese of Western America, Alhambra CA, 2017

Saints of Africa, Fr. Jerome Sanderson & Carla Thomas, MD, Christ the Savior Brotherhood Publishing, Indianapolis IN, 2006

Ancient African Christianity, David E Wilhite, Routledge Taylor & Francis Group, London & New York, 2017

Wade in the River: The Story of the African Christian Faith, Fr. Paisius Altschul, Crossbearers Publishing, Kansas City MO, 2001

Histories of the Monks of Upper Egypt, Paphnutius/Translation by Tim Vivian, Cistercian Publishing, Kalamazoo MI, 1993

Matericon: Instructions of Abba Isaiah to the Honorable Nun Theodora, Translation from Saint Theophan the Recluse, Saint Paisius Serbian Orthodox Monastery, Safford AZ, 2001

The Sayings of the Desert Fathers, Traslated by Benedicta Ward, Cistercian Publishing, Kalamazoo MI, 1975

The Roots of Nubian Christianity Uncovered: the Triumph of the Last Pharaoh, Salim Faraji, Africa World Press, Trenton NJ/London/Cape Town, 2012

Orthodox Church of America, www.oca.org/saints/lives

ABOUT THE AUTHOR

FR. DEACON JOHN R. GRESHAM, JR.

DEACON JOHN is a native of King William County, VA and a graduate of Virginia State University. He studied at the Virginia Union University School of Theology and was the pastor of Trinity Baptist Church, West Point. He converted to Orthodox Christianity in 2014 and completed the St. Stephen's Certificate in Orthodox Theology from the Antiochian House of Studies in 2018. The same year, John was Ordained to the Holy Diaconate by His Grace Bishop Thomas.

Deacon John serves at the Saint Basil the Great parish in Hampton, VA where he is also a Teen SOYO advisor. He has served on the national board of the Fellowship of St. Moses the Black. He is a Ranger at York River State Park in Williamsburg and Membership Staffer at the Greater West Point YMCA. Deacon and Shamassy Brenda have been married for 30 years and reside in West Point.

Read more of Fr. Deacon John's writings at the All Saints West Point blog: https://all-saints-wp.org/

ABOUT THE COVER ARTIST

STEVE PRINCE | ARTIST, EDUCATOR, ART EVANGELIST

STEVE PRINCE is a native of New Orleans, Louisiana, and currently resides in Williamsburg, Virginia. Prince was born and raised Catholic from kindergarten through college. He received his BFA from Xavier University of Louisiana and his MFA in Printmaking and Sculpture from Michigan State University. He is the Director of Engagement and Distinguished Artist in Residence at the Muscarelle Museum of Art at William and Mary University. He has created several public and private commissions nationally and he has received numerous honors for his art and scholarship including the 2020 International Engage Art Contest Visual Art Grand Prize Winner, and the 2010 Teacher of the Year for the City of Hampton. Prince has shown his art internationally in various solo, group, and juried exhibitions.

He is an accomplished lecturer and workshop conductor in both sacred and secular settings internationally through a variety of media. In 2019 he worked with over 500 people to create a collective art piece focusing on the history of chattel slavery stemming from the first documented Africans arriving on the shores of Point Comfort in 1619. His project was called Links which metaphorically championed the inextricable connections we have as human beings. Prince spreads a message of hope and renewal to the global community. His philosophy is derived from the cathartic Jazz funerary tradition in New Orleans, Louisiana called the Dirge and Second Line. Conversely, the Dirge represents the everyday issues and pains we confront and endure, whereas the Second Line represents new life, restoration, salvation, and yearning for the eternal while we are still alive.

See more from Steve Prince on his website:
https://steveprincestudio.com/

ABOUT THE ILLUSTRATOR

ANDREW KINARD

A SENIOR DevOps software engineer by day, Park End Books Associate Editor Andrew Kinard has practiced traditional Byzantine panel iconography for a decade, studying with masters from Greek, Romanian, Russian, and Bulgarian iconography traditions. In adapting traditional iconographic line drawings for the chapter headings, Andrew sought to highlight the African elements in the representations of the saints depicted with details like real First Century Lybian textile patterns on Simon of Cyrene's robes.

MORE FROM PARK END BOOKS

PARK END BOOKS is a traditional small press bringing to market accessible Christian education curricula and emerging Orthodox, Catholic, and other creedal Christian authors. Visit us at: ParkEndBooks.com

LETTERS FOR PILGRIMAGE:
LENTEN MEDITATIONS FOR TEEN GIRLS
By Sarah Lenora Gingrich and A. N. Tallent
Embark on the adventure of Lent armed for the journey!
From women who have survived the wilderness of life arrives this guide to the wilderness of Lent for teen girls. Learn from adventurous women who know how to wield a sword, cook over open flames, and work out their salvation in fear and trembling in this epistolary devotional covering Orthodox Lent, Holy Week, and Bright Week.

NORTHERN LIGHTS OF CHRIST:
LESSONS ON FAITH FROM ABOVE THE BIRCH LINE
By Nic Hartmann
"Finally, a book that provides real meaning for those looking to actually understand Nordic living." -Melissa Naasko, author of *Fasting as a Family* & *Hospitality for Healing* (Park End Books, 2022)

Travel with folklorist Nic Hartmann across the intersection between Nordic customs and Orthodox Christian faith in this perfect conversation starter for your fall and winter gatherings. Book clubs will love implementing the customs in these pages as they join together for cozy, nurturing, balancing, and edifying discussions about five Nordic values: Hygge, Koselig, Lagom, Sisu, and Isbiltur.

DARKNESS IS AS LIGHT:
CHRISTIAN WOMEN'S DEVOTIONS FOR PERSISTING IN HARD PLACES
By Twenty-Two Orthodox, Catholic, and Saint-Loving Christian Women; Edited by Summer Kinard
"Each entry sings with one theme: Christ is present. And it is this present God we can trust to sustain us, draw us closer, and sanctify us, no matter what." -*Sojourners Magazine*

In the beautifully illustrated and highly acclaimed devotional Darkness is as Light, twenty-two Christian women bear witness in order to help readers see God with them in suffering, recognize hope in the hardest of experiences, and learn to reach sideways in the darkness to those companions who are alongside them in their struggles.

COMING SOON FROM PARK END BOOKS

HOSPITALITY FOR HEALING
By Melissa Naasko
Care for the sick with wisdom and proven recipes based on convalescent cookbooks and the traditions of monastic infirmaries.

Seasoned with the warmth and wisdom she experienced in her abuela's kitchen, Matushka Melissa Naasko brings together the healing traditions of early 20th Century convalescent cookbooks and the long tradition of healing customs in monastic infirmaries. With the practicality readers have come to expect from her popular cookbook Fasting as a Family and her workshops, Mat. Melissa highlights what it means to help others recuperate in a time when new and chronic illnesses are more common than ever.

PARK END BOOKS